The Coronovirus

WHEN STAYING AT HOME HURTS TOO

How to overcome depression, frustration and anxiety

A National Treasure

For Conference or Speaking engagements, Contact:

Dr. Benita Paschel

Email: thepureinheartseesgod@gmail.com ❤

Phone: 205-434-0168

Dedication

This book is dedicated to everyone, especially those who are affected by the Coronovirus epidemic. I pray that it would give you guidance and healing during such a time as this.

FOREWORD

Today, everyone is affected by the Coronovirus epidemic directly or indirectly. Many have lost their lives. Some are at home or in the hospital fighting to live to see another day. Family and friends are grieving over the loss of loved ones. It's so unfair and no one want to take the blame. Every nation is suffering. Hospitals are full of the sick. Yet, many are afraid to go to the hospital for fear of being injected or falsely tested for the Covid-19. Doctors, nurses and other medical staff members have lost their lives, in an effort to save others.

We all have been told that the Coronovirus started in China, but China deny these accusations. Some say the United States knew about it, but our country's leaders didn't take it serious. I've even heard the virus started with experimenting with bats, etc. We've been told that some of the symptoms are nausea, high fevers, shortness of breath, flu like and pneumonia symptoms. Regardless, no one wants it! My question is where is the cure? Who cares about how it started? Yes, we care. Our main concern is: If this virus was created, then we know the creators of this virus should also have the formula to end it.

People don't know what to think. They've lost trust in world leaders. Their faith is being tried right now, but there is still hope. Churches all over the world are being closed. Many leaders have resulted to social media. Although this is an alternative, some people don't know how to worship or praise God at home. Businesses have closed or suffered. Still the rich want more. In spite of, there's always an answer. As you read my book, allow God to guide and reveal Himself to you more personally.

PRAYER

Dear Lord, we come to you with humble hearts thanking you first for watching over us and giving us another day to worship you. Thank you for creation and all the blessings that surrounds us. Thank you for being an awesome God (Yahweh) one that we can depend on, an everlasting father of Truth and honor. We thank you for your Spirit and wisdom, for her beauty radiates. To behold your creation, your breath of life and essence is awesome. Thank you for your son Jesus (Yeshua the Christ). His atonement and blood on Calvary's cross forgives us of sins. Because of this, we ask that you forgive us of our every wrongdoing and hearken to our prayer as we join in unity this day and plead our cause.

Father, you are the True God, the Omnipotent, the Omniscient and the Omnipresent one who sees and knows all things. You see all justice and injustices everywhere. Dear God, you are the author of good and it is never in your heart to hurt your children. Although things are permitted, your judgment is fair and no one can ever surpass reaping what they have sowed. Father, cruelty and sin have taken over the nation. The greatest to the least of us have strayed from your will. Therefore, a Coronovirus plague has swept the nation, killing both good and evil people. Father we plead for your mercy. Can't nobody heal the nation but you God. Please blow your healing breath on all of us. Let us feel your power like those on the Day of Pentecost. This way all Nations would know that it is you and turn back to fear and worship you.

Yahweh, through Yeshua we obtain this mercy as we witness the whole nation cry out to you. Lord, we don't know the beginning or ending of this virus epidemic, nor do we know the ending of the sex trafficking, the murders and other sins that the rebellious cause everywhere. Lord you know how to end it. Oh Father we ask that you prepare your children's heart to get right. We ask that you protect the just and give us more time to minister your word to those who are unjust, even in our families. Remove these plagues from us and allow the sun of your Glory to shine again. Father, help the ignorant, the dumb, the unbelieving, and the lost to understand who you are. Father, show them your love light. Convert them Father. Give them a special testimony so that others will become your disciples. We thank you for answering our prayers, in Yeshua the Christ's name we pray – Amen.

Mental Health

Your right now thought, how your senses operate, your ideas, your being, your gestures, your emotions, behaviors, etc., all has to do with your mental health. There's no way around it. It can be defined as life. You can't walk unless your brain can comprehend and tell you what to do. There's another attachment that goes with it. It is called physical health. I will elaborate on it briefly, then go back to my mental health topic. This is because both are opposite of each other and fits like a glove.

Physical Health has a lot to do with how you nourish and take care of your body. Your daily exercise, proper meal intake, vitamins, taking care of your hygiene, etc. It is essential that all of us take heed and do these things, because it strengthens our body, and assure that we stay healthy. This way we can produce good red and white blood cells. Our blood can flow smoother, ridding blood clots. We need strong muscles.

Problems arrive when we don't properly take care of our physical health. When this happens your body begin to deteriorate. Many have hypertension, diabetes, heart disease, etc. A lot of it stems from diet intake. Foods with too much cholesterol, sodium, saturated fats, etc. There's a saying that goes, "Its not how much you eat, it's what you eat." In other words, there are people who eat several meals a day with the right ingredients. However, a person can eat one meal and it may have more calories than all the several meals combined.

When your body fails, it messes with your emotions. For instance, excessive weight gain can cause lack of self- confidence. This can cause you to have stress, that can build up over periods of time. If you step on a nail, it affects your physical health. It may also cause you to cry. All of this can cause stress because your body reacts to sudden changes. Many times these changes affect you over long periods of time. It can drain you and cause frustration, agony, even anger. You can become disgusted with others and yourself, if decisions you have made alters your life's scheduled plans and cause unforeseen mental health issues. Therefore, your body's physical health ignites your mental health, which causes it to communicate your senses, behaviors and emotions.

Mental health issues can disrupt your normal routine and even cause you to be unhappy. Your sleeping habits may change. You may even find yourself withdrawn from friends. It can build or tear down relationships. According to HHS (2020) "Mental health includes our emotional, psychological, and social well-being. It affects how we think, feel, and act. It also helps determine how we handle stress, relate to others, and make choices. Mental health is important at every stage of life, from childhood and adolescence through adulthood."

Mental Health issues may also be hereditary. Problems are not always caused by physical defects or issues due to malnutrition. Mental issues can be caused by abuse, whether physical, emotional or sexual. Ones upbringing and environment can have a great impact on whether a person undergo psychological changes. Other mental disorders may include psychosis, schizophrenia, bipolar, major depression, etc. In such cases, these people are normally supervised by doctors and are prescribed medication to help them stay on course. These are considered major life-threatening mental health conditions.

Chapter I

HOME

There's a saying that goes, "Home is where the heart is." We all love the place we call our home. It's where we're comfortable and feel safe. We live there and sleep there. We raise our children there. It's our castle, our nest and where we can have peace of mind. We are the dictators of when to come and go as we please at our own home. What happens when someone tells you, stay at home and don't come outside? Instantly, you become a prisoner in your own home. Perhaps, you may begin to understand how those who are incarcerated really feel.

The Covid-19 epidemic has swept the nation and invaded our rights as human beings to live in a normal environment that God created for all of us to experience on a daily basis. It is where the sun shines, the wind blows, the flowers bloom, the birds fly, the trees bend as they put out oxygen. We see colors, shapes, people, and experience what we have always taken for granted, until we lose it. It's like having a home, you lose it, then become homeless living on the streets. That's a hard fall. That homeless person desires shelter, love, peace, a job, clothing and food. Can you imagine their pain?

The person with a home can become homeless in their own home. Why? It is because your environment to go and come as you please is also your home. Being able to work and pay your bills to keep what you have is vitally important. What happens when you can't? What happens when your world leaders tell you to come outside only to shop for food, but you must be inside at a certain time. You're alienated from your closest family and friends for fear of getting sick. Here, many cannot handle this burden. Some have committed suicide already, because FREEDOM to them cannot be a dictatorship. It's either die happy or live to fear the unexpected. Nevertheless, for those who refuse to give up, live to see the next happy moment.

Boredom

Looking at the same people and walls everyday can be challenging. This is the real test of your heart. You will discover where your true shortcomings are and whether you're able to tolerate the unexpected. This is the time you need to be more creative and switch things up. Change the scenery in your home. Add color. Try new recipes. Explore different television networks. You cannot sit around your home, sobbing over the Coronovirus televised broadcasts. It will only hurt you. Yes, heed the warnings but never allow it to control your happiness. Appreciating your family and being grateful is the only way to overcome boredom. Boredom cause too much mischievous explorations and failures, because people tend to act without thought. Connecting with family and embracing yourself defines who you are. Believing in yourself, what motivates you and personal fulfillment can sustain you during time of misery and boredom. You've got to explore your inward creative talents and avail them to the people you love. It brings happiness, refreshing and longevity.

Children

It's easy for small children to be affected with boredom. For them to sit still is like asking wind to stop blowing. During this challenge it's very import for you to ask them what they want to do. As parents, offer suggestions.   After you tell them about the Coronovirus and its affects, allow your children to tell you how they would handle it. Ask them what they want to watch on television. Let the kids tell you how they want to study their homework. Allow the children to tell you how they want to communicate with their friends. Let the children tell you what they would like to eat. Let them tell you how they want their room decorated. No, I'm not saying that parents would agree with everything their kid dictates. I'm simply asking the parent to allow their children to use their creativity to help overcome potentially stressful moments. The parents are the final organizers and know the limits. This helps to harmonize the family and rid unwanted stressors in the home.

Children burn a lot of energy. They like to run, ride their bikes, play with friends, etc. If this is taken away, their livelihood diminishes and they become depressed. Now, you have a mental health issue. What kids have more than anyone is vivid imagination and creativity. As adults, you must not forget. You must take your minds back to your teacher's classroom. Do you remember the pictures you painted? Do you remember the nice cards and pictures that you drew? You ran home excited to show your parents. As a child, it meant the world to you, because it was the creative expression of who you are. Therefore, when a child express themselves, it releases positive energy, shapes their destiny and motivates them to do greater things.

Teenagers

On the other hand, teenagers are different. They are already struggling to find their own new identity. They wrestle with, the questions, who am I and what do I want unaware? Girls breast enlarges. Boys penis grows. Some seek to explore their sexual feelings, which is a part of growing up. There is peer pressure, the dare to try new drugs, smoke a cigarette, skip school, sneak out the house or hold secrets. I know this sounds kind of sketchy, but it's not. It's the reality of knowing that a teenager's regular pressures of life with the added Stay-at-home Coronovirus scenario is double trouble. So, the question is, what do you do from here?

It's not going to always be fun dealing with half-grown kids who believe their advice is the best. Please know that it is with good intentions. First, know that a teenager's happiness dictates how well they do in school and connect with others in their home. They cannot be smothered. Their thoughts are always evolving. Yes, there's a lot on their minds. So, make sure you handle them carefully. If not, as a parent you may become confused and misinterpret the true meaning of how your child is defining themselves. So, listen attentively and watch with caution.

Teenagers are gatherers of information. They like learning new things, exploring social media and current issues about up-to-date clothing fashions, new songs, updates about celebrities, etc. This put them in certain moods and allow them to feel and connect with their own genres. Allow them to do so. Destiny always have its way of altering and/or correcting itself with time.

Teenagers like to express their truth. Even if they are wrong, you must allow their truth to be understood by them, even if they are corrected. If not, you can lose them at an early age. The best way for parents to gain their teenagers trust is to share some of your mistakes and tell them how you corrected it. Most important, is to help them to understand how it was unhealthy for you. Allow your teenager to express what route they may have taken in your same situation and why. Teenagers like to analyze things and it makes them feel a sense of pride and self-confidence. If you take this route, it helps your child to think through situations before they make a decision.

The worst thing a parent can do is pretend to be perfect. Just like parents watch teenagers, they are watching you too. Communication and understanding the process of a teenager's growth as changes are made in the home are vitally important. As a parent, don't portray yourself as your teenager's friend. You are their parent and have to be strong. As a parent, assign them duties of greater responsibility, but utilize it where they can feel free to be themselves. For example, Martha has to clean the kitchen within one hour, but she can listen to her favorite music while doing so. Martha has to babysit for three hours, but she can watch her favorite movie with earphones on, as long as her baby sister is sitting next to her watching Barney with her own iPad and headphones. Martha must study and do all of her homework assignments without outside distractions. Once completed, she can have an hour of quality time to talk with her friends before bedtime. In other words, make room and allow your growing teenager to develop themselves naturally.

Parents

Being a mother and father is like moving into a new home with all of your belongings placed into one room. You have to sort it out and find out who it belongs to, what drawer or closet to place it in. Put all the furniture in the right room, the food in the refrigerator too. Then parents have to care for themselves, their children, make all the final decisions, pay all the bills, take care of the pets - all of it! Yet, it has to balance like a checkbook. They are the role-models in the home. If anything go wrong, things can shatter like glass. Broken, crushed, dangerous or even life-threatening situations can occur when parents are unorganized.

The At-Home Covid-19 effect has really altered ways a parent may do things. With the loss of jobs and income, more stress is added. Now, parents are more worried about their children. Nevertheless, parents must remain calm and cheerful, while seeking ways to better their situation at all times. They must seek out organizations and resources to help carry the load during these perilous times.

The greatest test in the home would be parents becoming bored with each other. You wake up to the same face all day in the home together, go to sleep at night, then it revolves. Well, you may as well utilize this time to think about how you can spice things up. Reflect and re-encounter your dating moments. Everyday you have to relive this moment and to renew your vows to one another daily would be great. It's not about the fancy dress, the diamond ring, the dance or the cake. It's whether or not you can pass the test when real pressure come to test your vows, commitments and faithfulness to each other. The test of true responsibility and strength when opposition strikes, speak loud. Would you be able to stand and fight that battle, or would you give up and run?

Realize that the bitter and sweet rolls just like the wheat and tares grow. You cannot have one without the other. Responsibility is always first, even if bad times cause you to sell a wedding ring, a wedding dress, or your favorite car to feed your family. I'm hoping this is not the case, but sacrificing to help your family is never an option. It's always prevalent.

Romance has its way of making babies when there's a lot of time at home. This Stay-at-home agenda would probably bring numerous births the year of 2020-2021. There may be candlelight dinners, sweet perfumes, laced gowns, and moments when you need your companion to embrace you to relieve stress. However, parents must use caution and protection or you can end up with a baby during one of the worst times in history. Yes, babies are beautiful. Yet, there is no guarantee that the hospital can save a newborn baby from the Coronovirus. The virus is everywhere. Just like people are dying, babies are born everyday into a society of uncertainty and chaos. So, I say to parents to love each other. Keep up the romance, but use good judgement and make decisions that would help to sustain and keep you flourishing, not tear you down.

I highly recommend that parents continue to find ways to communicate with the family as a whole. Eat breakfast, lunch and dinner together. Take turn eating your favorite meals. Watch family movies, comedy would be very helpful. Most important, pray together. Prayer reveals the heart. It restores, give hope, cleanses and purify thoughts.

DEPRESSION, FRUSTRATION, ANXIETY
Chapter II

People everywhere experience things that cause them to give up, worry or even commit suicide. It's a time when they may feel all hope is lost or no one cares. Life bring the ups and downs. We all like the ups and good moments, but the downs stinks and has a lot to do with attitude. Your attitude is reflected by your inner confidence of knowing who you are, and the desire to overcome situations no matter how difficult times may get. You have to be your own motivator. Why? The person who shaped your confidence or molded you may not be around. Therefore, your next mood, thought or action can make you or break you.

Depression

Depression is not always noticeable or understood. It is easily denied because people don't like the term mental health. The word mental does not mean that you are crazy or have a deficiency. It simply means your well-being, having the ability to think, make decisions and understand that your own capabilities are important. It goes hand-in-hand with physical health. Both are vitally important. Even if you are hurt physically, it affects you mentally. Physical pain and/or limitations can halt where you go, or cause stressors, especially if you lost an arm, a leg or just experiencing joint pain.

Depression can affect people in different ways. Some may have suicidal thoughts, while others may overeat, feel helpless or sad. You may feel down or lost. It may appear to others as laziness. It's not, you just have to realize that depression is knocking on your door. The loss of interest in one's favorite hobbies, life's legacies or goals are some alerts. If you see any of these signs in yourself or your loved ones, please do not take it lightly. Get some help. Early intervention may help stop disability or even save a life.

Depression can be amongst persons who are financially stressed. It can be someone who just got laid off, got fired from their job, or just don't make enough to care for their family. When their emotions kick in, you may find them staring off in long gazes. They may not want to go outside or even participate in regular exercising routines. Some may call it lazy. It's not laziness. It's a sickness. As indicated earlier, one that is often denied and overlooked. It has to be treated.

There are different levels of depression where doctors may label you as being disabled. For instance, major depression such as suicidal thoughts, isolation and loss of interest in hobbies can be very detrimental. It is treatable with medication and counseling. The only problem is that the victim must admit that they are vulnerable and depression exists. Many are in denial and think what they are experiencing is a normal part of life. They may not wake up until it's too late.

That's when they have failed marriages, have lost loved ones and friends due to overreacting, or by doing and saying the unusual.

Some mental health medical patients are seen by psychiatrists, clinical counselors and/or psychologists. Depression can cause someone to be bipolar. You may have mood swings, mixed emotions, suicidal thoughts, tantrums, etc. This sickness can last the rest of your life. It is often triggered as a result of overly extending yourself beyond what you can bare, not taking your medication or not listening to your doctor's advice. It can be family inherited. This is why medical applications ask whether anyone in your family have these issues, which may include heart disease, hypertension, etc. It doesn't stop here and can worsen. There is also psychosis. This is where you may have loss of memory or reality connection. You may become supervised by others, have dementia or other life-changing experiences. Many in this category are elderly and are often supervised by other family members. Sometimes family members hire caregivers to assist, while they work regular jobs to care for their own immediate family.

Depression is not just for adults and the elderly. Children are victims too. That child who is bullied by other children may appear to be sad all the time or even show signs of aggression at home. Many parents overlook the symptoms. Your child's grades may suffer. You may notice isolation, weight loss or weight gain. They may even change hobbies and their character may become questionable. This is the time to ask questions, to do research and follow-up. Visiting your child's school, talking to their teacher and/or friend's parents could answer some of your questions. The best method to understanding your child is through bonding and relationship. You have to present yourself as a parent and a friend. Why? Children talk to their friends more than their parents, because friends don't invade their private space. They talk and share experiences. Whereas, parents intervene. Therefore, being approachable and trusted by your child can secure a very long-lasting parent/child union. This way, the child can talk and express themselves, without hypocrisy.

Frustration

Frustration is what I call an additive. It's an ingredient hidden with the main recipe, but is always on the main surface to be visually seen by way of facial expressions. It's the ingredient that flares attitude and behavior. It can cause a person to say and do what they could regret the rest of their lives. It's normally surfaces when a person has not fulfilled their goal, accomplished success or able to do what their heart desires.

Sometimes life can bring uncertainties, such as the Coronovirus epidemic. A business owner may have been at the peak of their business success, but it declined when customers were lost and the shop had to be closed. Can you imagine all the hard work, time and money invested, just to see it go downhill again? What about going to work twelve long hours, but when you get home dinner is not prepared? Frustration deals with your emotions and thoughts. Too much disappointment leads to behavior change. Then your behavior change cause action. Action cause consequences, good or bad.

Being able to accept failures can be hard, especially if it was not caused by you. You must seek alternative ways to get back on track and ways to cope with it. Sometimes it's not easy. Nevertheless, you have to press your way through uncertainty whether or not you understand it. It's a process. The process consist of decisions, change and adjustment. It's not going to always be about you. It could be the situation that hinders your progress. You then have to make up your mind whether you're ready to move past that situation. You have to press your way. You have to change your attitude, environment or even social circle. To be healthy mentally and emotionally calls for intelligent decisions. You must remember that you are not the only one who are affected by what happens in your life. Think about your parents, spouse, children, friends, even your pet. Yes, pets can also feel your pain and agony.

Everyone in their lifetime can become frustrated. A student can be frustrated when he or she does not have enough study time and fail their exam. A vocalist becomes frustrated when their voice cracks on stage. How about when people all over the world had to adjust to the death of Michael Jackson, or even the loss of their best friend? To break out and have that freedom to be you without hesitation, limitations and being happy are without question. Soldiers in the military who desire to come home, but have to fight a war and don't know if they would ever return home can be very frustrated.

Depending on the situation, many may never get the counseling they need to overcome these oppositions or barriers. Therefore, to vent with your pastor, a best friend, your parents, role model or mentor can be priceless. So, it's important that you choose your circle of people who represent you as a person. It has a lasting affect on your life. It is my recommendation that everyone consult with a professional counselor at least three times in their lifetime. As a child age 10, next would be age 30 middle years, to see how far you have come. Then age 60, to assure mental stability for yourself and to share your hopes and dreams that you have been prayerful about concerning your family and friends.

Anxiety

Have you ever wanted to do something so fast, or accomplish a task expeditiously that you lost sight on a more important one? Have you ever wanted to get somewhere real fast, that you went over the speed limit or perhaps ran a stop sign? Have you ever wanted to meet a deadline and took the wrong path and ended up back where you started? This is anxiety. It can be accompanied by excessive worrying, fatigue, emotional distress, crying, etc. People with anxiety may become mentally disoriented if their issues are not controlled. However, anxiety can be dissolved if a person can recognize it and take steps to rectify it. Ways to overcome anxiety may include a healthy diet, proper sleep (8 hours per night recommended), good exercise, a support group, or supportive family or friends. I also recommend healthy activities, social gatherings, perhaps a nice family vacation, as being a great way to release anxiety, frustration, stress and depression.

Anxiety can be caused by stress. It could be due to overthinking or overextending yourself. Perhaps you feel anxiety right before you go to the doctor. How about when you want something to be perfect, but fear that you may make a mistake, like hitting a home run at a softball game or winning a 100 yard dash. Anxiety do not always have to be a medical condition. It can also be a normal process that we all go through in similar situations.

WORSHIPPING GOD DURING TRIALS

Chapter III

There's a saying that goes, "Trials Come to Make you Strong". My question to you is, Was it you? What kind of trials are you going through right now? Many trials come and go. How you allow that trial to affect you may define you as a person. Everybody's trials are different. Each trial influence your character and relationship with others. Believe it or not, your trial affect others too. This is how things evolve. It's a circle that has no end. Everybody has a cycle. If you are in a person's circle, a lifelong thought pattern, behavior and emotions will forever embrace you. However, only you can make that change. You are the one who has to end that circle. This is why you have to be very careful of the company you keep, your environment and associations.

We all grew up in different cultures. We learn things. We may see things differently, hear things differently, or even worship differently. Yet, we are uniquely made according to our purpose and how we manifest ourselves to others on this beautiful planet called, earth. As we continue to live, we adapt to changes in society and hope to see the next day evolve.

What We Believe

No two people believe the same. It is because no one else can be you. God has His beginning and finishing touch. People may believe in the same God or higher power, but our personal relationship with Him is different. Why? It is because we all do different things, our looks are different, our lifestyles are different, our thoughts are different. We are all held accountable for the things that we say and do. It is what makes us who we are.

Many of us believe things based upon how we were raised as children. Our parents, grandparents, siblings, teacher and even church affiliations mold us into the person we are today. Nevertheless, there are some people who stray or change when they become adults. The change can be good or bad. Therefore, when trials come we act differently based upon how a trial makes us feel. Your belief, Spirituality, what you embrace as a power source has great influence on your life. If that source is about love, respect and forgiveness, then how you analyze and react to hurtful or devastating moments may be different from those whose belief is far from that.

Worship Experience

To open your mind and heart and allow God to penetrate your being is the greatest gift and reward that any person can ever experience. You reverence and praise the higher power who exists within you. Some cannot explain the magnitude and experience, because it is without words and man's comprehension. What they do know is there's nothing else that comes close to their higher power experience. This time is pure devotion. This is a praise and worship that eliminates everything and everybody from the outside and allow the flow of God's presence to take over.

Worship is normally done in different ways. Many pray, clap their hands, do joyful dances, sing songs of praise, moan, cry with tears of joy, etc. The reward is a closer union and/or relationship with God. During worship people often give thanks to God for all that he's done, including their requests to help deliver or protect them during their trials. Faith in their higher power ignites. It beautifies them, bring hope and confidence. Worship is a daily practice. It helps to sustain and teaches order and conformity.

Love Yourself

The person called you have a side that you can see and another side that you can see, but fail to see. First, let's take a look at your flesh. Yes, your outward appearance that you see. This is the side that you see with your natural visual eyes. This is your covering that you didn't ask for. It normally resemble other family members. It could be your mother, father, grandparents, or other siblings. No matter who you may look like, it is you.

Believe it or not, some people don't like what they see. Even as a child, there are some who do not feel beautiful. Many today feel like there could be improvement to their facial or body features. With children who lack self-confidence or self-assurance, they could be amongst those who are bullied. Sometimes it could go as far as committing suicide.

To love yourself goes far beyond what you see or know. There's also another side of you that's contained inside. The stuff that you do not see such as your soul and spirit. You also have that invisible heart, your instincts, and your thoughts. You have personality, behavior and other characteristics that shape you into the person you are today. Therefore, you cannot analyze yourself just by looking at your flesh. You must include God, your higher power and your inner person who tells the story about who you really are.

What are your secret thoughts? How do you treat yourself when no one else is watching you? When you're alone, what kind of thoughts go through your mind? What is your conversation like? What do you watch on television? Who is your inspiration? I ask all of these questions, because it tells a story about you. In that story, you can find out where your strength and flaws are. You build on your strengths, as long as it bring honor to yourself and others. Your flaws are those weaknesses, the embarrassing stuff that you want to hide from others. This means that you don't approve of it yourself, but have allowed it to linger due to procrastination of your own. This is when you have to wake up from your sleep and force yourself to improve. You have to do better for yourself or you may end up in a life-long crisis of no return.

To love yourself is to recognize who you are. Try to be your best self. It comes with admitting your faults. Improving and reaching higher everyday should be your primary goal. Each day bring change and commitment. You have to speak positive words to yourself. You are your own constant reminder. No one else can be you. No one else know you like you do. Focus on what it would be like if you were perfect. You may say that it's impossible. I say to you that all things are possible. You need to press your way. There are days when you may be tired and feel like giving up, but you have to follow the plan, by setting up a schedule, then be persistent. It may seem hard at first, but if you continue it gets easier. Then, finally you have arrived.

Respect Others

The golden rule is to love your neighbor as yourself and treat others as you would want to be treated. It is also Bible Scripture. This is Truth. It will bring you long life, peace, honor and integrity. The Bible and these words are to be lived by each and everyday. I even recommend the Ten (10) Commandments. If everyone lived accordingly, this world would be a much better place to live. I know that all people do not believe in God. Yet, I say it doesn't take people believing in God to have what the elders call, "Common Sense". We all have a mind. Unless you are mentally retarded and cannot think for yourself, then you should know better.

We are all born with God's essence. He created us all. His breath is eternal, pure and just. Because of this, we share what He is made of. Therefore, we are led and guided by His Spirit, His voice. We have convictions. If we do not take heed when He, (the Spirit) warns us, then we have disobeyed. So, I believe in my heart that if people wanted to do good, they can. If they don't want to, it is because it is their choice.

I grew up in a small country town, south Alabama. Here, my parents taught me and my other siblings to say Yes ma'am, Yes sir and No ma'am, No Sir, to the elders. We always said Thank you and May I. This was mandatory. We were raised and chastised by community mothers and fathers back in the day. They told us stories, provided guidance and wisdom for us to cherish throughout our lifetime. Grandparents were MuDears' and Big Mamas, those who labored morning to sunset, caring for their grandchildren. We appreciated them, because they were the backbone in every family.

Today, many changes have taken place. In the news I see the elderly abused, raped or murdered by the younger generation. It hurts my heart. It appears that the newer generation is lacking so much wisdom and guidance. I try to understand everybody's role and where they all went wrong. I then realized that every decade there are new discoveries, upgrades and changes with technology and information. This does not necessarily mean that what is imparted into their learning is beneficial. Nevertheless, the older generation must also learn and/or adapt to change in order to reach a generation of youths, or they may remain lost.

People everywhere life's journey may have a different interpretation than yours. This is expected. However, the basic principles of life such as caring, sharing and treating others as valuable human beings are expected. No matter who people are, we are all distinct, beautiful and magnificent beings who share this earth to fulfill our calling and purpose. Therefore, let's learn from one another. Be the magnet that draw others to be compelled to do that which is good.

References

U.S. Department of Health and Human Services, (2020). Let's talk about it. *What is Mental Health?* Retrieved from, https://www.mentalhealth.gov/basics/what-is-mental-health

QUESTIONS FOR THOUGHT

1. What is the difference between mental and physical health?

2. Why is it so important to eat a well-balanced meal on a daily basis?

3. What is stress and how does it interfere with your daily activities?

4. What is depression? Have you ever been depressed? If so, how did you overcome it?

5. What is frustration? What kind of things or situations make you encounter such?

6. What is anxiety? What do you want to do right now that requires patience?

7. What is Covid-19? What are you doing to make sure that it does not harm you or others?

8. What belief strengthens you everyday and why?

ABOUT THE AUTHOR

Dr. Benita Paschel is an inspiring pastoral counselor and entrepreneur whose goal is to help heal people that go through everyday challenges. She is very compassionate and dedicated to her work. Also known as Benita (Truth) because of her straightforwardness, she accepts this honor as a way to continuously stay genuine and/or authentic to her call. Dr. Benita Paschel has over thirty (30) years of ministry, customer resolution and patient care experience. She has a Masters and Doctoral Degree in Theology with a major in Pastoral Counseling. In addition, Dr. Benita has a Bachelors Degree in Human Services and is currently attending school to complete her Masters Degree in Human Services as well.

Dr. Benita grew up in the country, on the Southside of Alabama. She has humble beginnings. Raised to love and respect all people, her church upbringing are without question. Her devotion as a praise and worship leader led her to seek other roles of influence. Her call into the ministry at an early age is what has inspired her to do what she is doing now.

Today, she has a beautiful family and are thanking Yahweh everyday for such gratefulness. As she continues on her journey, she would like to be a blessing to all that God sends her way. A light and river that refresh and cleanses people's hearts would always be the energy Dr. Benita needs to stay motivated to the Call, that God has placed upon her life.